FINDING
YOUR
TRIBE
A GUIDE TO ANCESTRY, GENEALOGY, AND FAMILY HISTORY
MARCEL DEER

I0782717

FINDING YOUR TRIBE

A Guide to Ancestry, Genealogy, and Family
History

Marcel Deer

Table of Contents

Picture this: You're sitting at a family gathering, listening to your great-aunt recount stories of ancestors you've never heard of before. Names, dates, and places fill your mind, but you can't quite piece together how it all fits into your family's story. You're intrigued, but the prospect of diving into genealogy research seems overwhelming. Where do you even start?

I've been there. A few years ago, I found myself in that exact position—fascinated by my family's history but daunted by the mountain of information to sift through. Fast-forward to today and I've not only traced my lineage back several generations but also uncovered incredible stories that have fundamentally changed how I view my place in the world.

Here's the kicker: I did it all in my spare time without becoming a full-time family historian or spending a fortune on research. In this book, I will show you exactly how I did it and how you can do the same - or better.

Welcome to "Finding Your Tribe: A Guide to Ancestry, Genealogy, and Family Historyt." In these pages, you'll discover:

- How to kickstart your family history journey with just 4 hours a week
- The top free and low-cost tools that will 10x your research efficiency
- Insider tricks for breaking through stubborn brick walls in your family tree
- How to leverage cutting-edge AI and DNA technology to uncover hidden connections
- Strategies for preserving and sharing your discoveries to inspire future generations

Whether you're a complete novice or have dabbled in genealogy before, this book will equip you with the skills, strategies, and inspiration to uncover your family's unique story. Are you ready to embark on the adventure of a lifetime? Let's dive in.

Chapter 1: The Roots of Your Story

Welcome to the fascinating world of family history and genealogy! I'm thrilled you've picked up this book and are ready to embark on an incredible journey of self-discovery. As someone who has spent years researching my own family tree and helping others do the same, I can tell you that uncovering your ancestral roots is one of the most rewarding pursuits you can undertake.

But before we dive into the nitty-gritty of research techniques and DNA testing, let's take a moment to explore why tracing your family history matters in the first place. After all, with our busy modern lives, why should we care about long-dead relatives and dusty old records?

The Power of Knowing Your Story

Here's the thing - understanding where you come from gives you an invaluable sense of identity and belonging. It connects you to something larger than yourself and provides context for your place in the world. As the famous African proverb states, "To know where you're going, you must know where you've been."

When I first started researching my own family tree, I was amazed to discover ancestors who had lived through major historical events like the Civil War and the Great Depression. Suddenly, history came alive in a whole new way. I wasn't just reading about these events in textbooks anymore - I was imagining my own flesh and blood experiencing them firsthand.

Learning about your ancestors' triumphs and struggles can also be incredibly inspiring. Maybe you'll uncover a great-grandmother who was a pioneering female doctor or a great-uncle who immigrated to America with nothing but the clothes on his back and built a thriving business. Their stories of perseverance and courage can motivate you to push through your own challenges.

Did you know? Studies have shown that children who know more about their family history have higher self-esteem and a greater sense of control over their lives. Sharing ancestral stories creates a strong intergenerational bond.

Beyond the personal benefits, genealogy research contributes to the broader fields of history, anthropology, and genetics. By piecing together our individual family histories, we're helping to fill in the gaps of human migration patterns, cultural diffusion, and genetic inheritance. It's citizen science at its finest!

Getting Started: The Basics of Family Tree Research

Now that we've covered the "why," let's dive into the "how" of genealogy research. Don't worry if you're starting from scratch - everyone begins somewhere, and with the wealth of resources available today, it's easier than ever to get started.

The first step is to gather what you already know. Start by writing down basic information about yourself, your parents, and your grandparents. Names, birth dates, marriage dates, and places of residence are all valuable pieces of the puzzle. Ask older relatives for any family stories or documents they might have tucked away.

Next, you'll want to choose a system for organizing your research. While you can certainly use pen and paper, I highly recommend utilizing genealogy software or online family tree builders. These tools make it easy to input data, visualize relationships, and share your findings with others. Some popular options include:

- Ancestry.com
- FamilySearch.org (free)
- MyHeritage
- Findmypast

Whichever platform you choose, make sure to cite your sources as you go. Trust me, future you will thank present you for keeping meticulous records of where each piece of information came from.

Top Tip: Start with what you know and work backwards in time. It's tempting to jump straight to searching for that rumored royal ancestor, but building a solid foundation of recent generations will make your research much more accurate and rewarding in the long run.

The Detective Work Begins

Once you've input the information you already know, it's time to start digging deeper. Here are some key record types to look for:

1. Census records: Conducted every 10 years in many countries, these provide snapshots of households at specific points in time.
2. Vital records: Birth, marriage, and death certificates offer crucial details about life events.
3. Church records: Baptisms, marriages, and burials were often recorded by religious institutions.
4. Military records: Draft registrations, service records, and pension files can be goldmines of information.
5. Immigration records: Passenger lists, naturalization papers, and passport applications document your ancestors' journeys.
6. Newspapers: Obituaries, birth announcements, and local news items can add color to your family's story.

Many of these records are now available online through genealogy websites and digital archives. However, don't discount the value of visiting local courthouses, libraries, and historical societies in person. Sometimes the most exciting discoveries happen when you least expect them!

Did you know? The longest documented family tree in the world belongs to the Chinese philosopher Confucius. It spans over 80 generations and includes more than 2 million members!

Overcoming Roadblocks

As you delve deeper into your research, you're bound to hit some brick walls. Maybe you can't find a great-grandparent's birth record, or family lore doesn't match up with documented evidence. Don't get discouraged - these challenges are all part of the genealogy journey.

Here are some strategies for overcoming common roadblocks:

1. Expand your search: Look for alternate name spellings, search broader date ranges, and consider neighboring counties or parishes.
2. Follow the FAN principle: Research your ancestor's Friends, Associates, and Neighbors. These connections often lead to new clues.
3. Join genealogy forums and social media groups: Fellow researchers can offer fresh perspectives and may even be distant relatives!
4. Take a DNA test: Genetic genealogy can break through brick walls and connect you with living relatives who might have additional information.
5. Hire a professional: If you're truly stuck, consider enlisting the help of a professional genealogist for targeted research.

Remember, patience and persistence are key. Sometimes the breakthrough you need is just around the corner!

The Thrill of Discovery

There's nothing quite like the excitement of uncovering a long-lost piece of your family puzzle. Whether it's finding your great-great-grandmother's signature on a marriage certificate or discovering a newspaper article mentioning your ancestor's heroic deed, these moments make all the hard work worthwhile.

As you continue your genealogy journey, take time to savor these discoveries. Share them with your family, create scrapbooks or digital albums, and consider ways to preserve your findings for future generations.

In the next chapter, we'll explore how to take your research to the next level with DNA testing and advanced research techniques. But for now, I encourage you to start building your family tree using the basics we've covered. You never know what fascinating stories you might uncover!

Chapter Summary:

- Understanding your family history provides a sense of identity and connection to the past
- Start by gathering information you already know and organizing it in genealogy software
- Key record types include census records, vital records, church records, and military records
- Overcome research roadblocks by expanding your search, using the FAN principle, and considering DNA testing
- Celebrate your discoveries and share them with family members

Chapter 2: Cracking the Genetic Code

Welcome back, genealogy detectives! In the last chapter, we laid the groundwork for building your family tree using traditional research methods. Now it's time to add a powerful new tool to your arsenal: DNA testing.

The field of genetic genealogy has exploded in recent years, revolutionizing the way we explore our family histories. By analyzing your DNA, you can uncover ethnic origins, connect with living relatives, and even break through longstanding brick walls in your research. Let's dive into the fascinating world of genetic genealogy and learn how to harness its power for your family history journey.

Understanding DNA Testing for Genealogy

Before we get into the nitty-gritty of testing options, let's cover some basic genetics. You inherit your DNA from your parents, who inherited it from their parents, and so on. This means that your DNA contains genetic markers from your ancestors going back hundreds, even thousands of years.

There are three main types of DNA tests used in genetic genealogy:

1. Autosomal DNA (atDNA): This test examines DNA from all of your ancestral lines and can help you find matches with relatives out to about 5-6 generations. It's the most popular type of test for genealogy purposes.
2. Y-DNA: This test looks at the Y chromosome, which is passed down from father to son. It can

trace your direct paternal line back many
generations. Only males can take this test.
3. Mitochondrial DNA (mtDNA): This test examines
DNA inherited from your mother's maternal line.
Both males and females can take this test, but it
only traces your direct maternal lineage.

Most genealogy DNA tests focus on autosomal DNA, as it
provides the broadest range of information and potential matches.
However, Y-DNA and mtDNA tests can be valuable for specific
research goals.

Did you know? While humans share about 99.9% of their DNA
with each other, that 0.1% difference is enough to make each
person unique (except for identical twins). This is why DNA
testing can be so powerful for genealogy!

Choosing a DNA Testing Company

Several companies offer DNA testing for genealogy purposes. The
"Big Five" in the industry are:

1. AncestryDNA
2. 23andMe
3. MyHeritage DNA
4. FamilyTreeDNA
5. LivingDNA

Each company has its strengths and weaknesses, so it's worth
considering your specific goals before choosing a test. Here's a
quick rundown:

- AncestryDNA: Largest database of test-takers,
strong integration with family trees
- 23andMe: Offers health reports in addition to
ancestry information

- MyHeritage DNA: Good for finding international matches, especially in Europe
- FamilyTreeDNA: Only company offering all three types of DNA tests (atDNA, Y-DNA, mtDNA)
- LivingDNA: Provides detailed breakdown of British and Irish ancestry

Personally, I recommend starting with AncestryDNA or 23andMe due to their large databases, which increase your chances of finding matches. You can always transfer your raw DNA data to other companies later for additional analysis.

Top Tip: Watch for sales around holidays like Mother's Day, Father's Day, and Black Friday. DNA test kits are often significantly discounted during these times.

Taking the Test

Once you've chosen a company and ordered your kit, the testing process is surprisingly simple:

1. Register your kit online using the unique code provided.
2. Provide a DNA sample, usually by spitting into a tube or swabbing the inside of your cheek.
3. Mail your sample back to the company in the prepaid envelope.
4. Wait 3-8 weeks for your results to be processed.

While you're waiting, take some time to review the company's privacy policies and adjust your sharing settings if desired. Genetic genealogy involves sharing some of your DNA information with potential relatives, so it's important to understand and be comfortable with the process.

Interpreting Your Results

When your results arrive, you'll typically receive two main types of information:

1. Ethnicity Estimates: This is a breakdown of your genetic ancestry, usually presented as percentages from different regions around the world.
2. DNA Matches: A list of other test-takers who share DNA with you, indicating a potential genetic relationship.

Let's break these down further:

Ethnicity Estimates

Your ethnicity estimate is often the most immediately exciting part of your results. It's fascinating to see your ancestry visualized in colorful pie charts and maps. However, it's important to remember that these estimates are just that - estimates. They're based on comparing your DNA to reference populations and can vary between companies.

Don't be surprised if your ethnicity estimate doesn't perfectly match your known family tree. Remember, you inherit random portions of DNA from your ancestors, so your genetic ethnicity might not reflect your entire genealogical background. Additionally, these estimates get less precise the further back in time you go.

DNA Matches

This is where the real genealogical gold lies. Your DNA matches are other people who have taken the same test and share segments of DNA with you, indicating a common ancestor. Matches are typically categorized by their estimated relationship to you, such as "2nd-3rd cousin" or "4th-6th cousin."

To make the most of your DNA matches:

1. Start with your closest matches and work your way down the list.
2. Look for familiar surnames and locations that align with your known family tree.
3. Reach out to matches who seem promising. Many are happy to collaborate and share information.
4. Use the shared matches feature to identify clusters of relatives who might be related through a common ancestor.

Did you know? On average, you share about 50% of your DNA with each parent, 25% with grandparents and siblings, 12.5% with first cousins, and so on. This is why DNA testing can reliably identify close relatives but becomes less precise with more distant relationships.

Advanced DNA Techniques

Once you've gotten comfortable with the basics of your DNA results, there are several advanced techniques you can use to squeeze even more information out of your genetic data:

1. Chromosome Mapping: This involves tracking which segments of your chromosomes came from which ancestors. It can help you identify how you're related to DNA matches.
2. Triangulation: By finding three or more people who all match each other on the same DNA segment, you can infer that this segment likely came from a common ancestor.

3. X-DNA Analysis: The X chromosome follows a unique inheritance pattern that can provide additional clues about your ancestry.
4. Endogamy Research: If your ancestors came from a small, isolated population (like an island community or certain religious groups), you may need special techniques to interpret your DNA results accurately.
5. Y-DNA and mtDNA Haplogroups: These can provide information about your deep ancestral origins and migration patterns thousands of years ago.

These techniques can be complex, but there are many online resources and courses available to help you learn. The International Society of Genetic Genealogy (ISOGG) is an excellent place to start for in-depth information.

Ethical Considerations in Genetic Genealogy

As powerful as DNA testing can be for genealogy, it's important to consider the ethical implications:

1. Privacy: Your genetic data contains sensitive information. Be sure you're comfortable with how testing companies use and store your data.
2. Unexpected Findings: DNA testing can reveal family secrets, like unknown adoptions or misattributed parentage. Be prepared for potentially surprising results.
3. Consent: Consider the privacy of your relatives before sharing information about them with DNA matches.
4. Law Enforcement Use: Some companies allow law enforcement to access their databases for criminal investigations. Research each company's policies if this is a concern for you.

5. Genetic Discrimination: While laws like GINA in the US provide some protections, be aware of potential risks related to insurance or employment.

Integrating DNA with Traditional Research

DNA testing is a powerful tool, but it's most effective when combined with traditional genealogical research. Here's how to integrate the two:

1. Use DNA matches to confirm paper trail research.
2. Explore the family trees of your DNA matches to find common ancestors.
3. Test multiple family members to get a more complete picture of your genetic genealogy.
4. Use DNA evidence to break through brick walls in your traditional research.
5. Join DNA-focused genealogy groups to learn from others and stay up-to-date on new techniques.

Remember, DNA testing and traditional research are complementary tools. Neither is infallible on its own, but together they can help you build a robust and accurate family tree.

The Future of Genetic Genealogy

The field of genetic genealogy is evolving rapidly. Here are some exciting developments to watch for:

1. Improved Ethnicity Estimates: As reference populations grow and algorithms improve, ethnicity estimates will become more precise.
2. Medical Insights: While most genealogy tests don't provide health information, this may change as our understanding of genetics grows.

3. Ancient DNA: Advances in extracting and analyzing DNA from archaeological remains are providing new insights into human history and migration patterns.
4. Epigenetics: This emerging field studies how environmental factors can affect gene expression across generations.
5. AI and Machine Learning: These technologies are being applied to genetic genealogy to help identify patterns and relationships more efficiently.

As we wrap up this chapter, I hope you're feeling excited about the possibilities of genetic genealogy. Whether you're just starting out or have been researching your family history for years, DNA testing can open up new avenues of discovery and connection.

In the next chapter, we'll explore how to leverage online resources and databases to supercharge your genealogy research. But for now, why not take that DNA test you've been considering? You never know what fascinating insights about your ancestors might be hiding in your genes!

Chapter Summary:

- DNA testing for genealogy examines autosomal DNA, Y-DNA, and mitochondrial DNA
- Major testing companies include AncestryDNA, 23andMe, MyHeritage, FamilyTreeDNA, and LivingDNA
- Results typically include ethnicity estimates and DNA matches to potential relatives
- Advanced techniques like chromosome mapping and triangulation can provide deeper insights
- Consider the ethical implications of DNA testing, including privacy concerns and unexpected findings
- Integrate DNA results with traditional genealogical research for the most comprehensive family history

Chapter 3: Building Your Family Tree - From Sapling to Mighty Oak

Welcome to the exciting world of family tree building! In this chapter, we're going to transform you from a genealogy newbie into a confident family historian. Think of your family tree as a living, breathing entity that starts as a tiny sapling and grows into a majestic oak with your careful nurturing. Let's dive in and explore the tools and techniques that will help you cultivate your ancestral garden.

Laying the groundwork: Start with what you know

The journey of a thousand miles begins with a single step, and your genealogy journey starts with you. Grab a piece of paper or open your favorite note-taking app, and write down everything you know about your immediate family:

- Your full name, date of birth, and place of birth
- Your parents' names, dates of birth, and places of birth
- Your siblings' names, dates of birth, and places of birth
- Your grandparents' names, dates of birth, and places of birth (if known)

Don't worry if you don't have all this information – that's part of the fun of genealogy! You'll be filling in these blanks as you go along.

Did You Know? The longest documented family tree belongs to the Chinese philosopher Confucius. It spans over 80 generations and includes more than 2 million members!

Interviewing relatives: Mining family lore for genealogical gold

Now that you've jotted down what you know, it's time to tap into your family's collective memory. Interviewing relatives is like striking genealogical gold – you never know what treasures you might uncover. Here are some tips to make the most of your family interviews:

a) Prepare a list of questions in advance. Some great starter questions include:

- What do you know about our family's origins?
- Do you remember any stories about your grandparents or great-grandparents?
- Where did our family live before settling in our current location?

b) Use props to jog memories. Old photos, heirlooms, or even a family recipe can spark recollections.

c) Record the conversation (with permission) so you can focus on the discussion rather than taking notes.

d) Be patient and respectful. Some family stories might be sensitive or painful to recall.

e) Follow up on interesting leads. If Aunt Mildred mentions a long-lost cousin in Australia, make a note to investigate further.

Pro Tip: Create a "genealogy go-bag" with a portable scanner, voice recorder, and notebook. You never know when an impromptu family gathering might turn into a goldmine of information!

Organizing your findings: The art of the family group sheet

As you gather information, you'll need a system to keep everything organized. Enter the family group sheet – a genealogist's best friend. A family group sheet is a form that records information about a nuclear family unit: parents and their children. Here's how to create one:

a) Start with the father's information: full name, date and place of birth, date and place of marriage, date and place of death (if applicable).

b) Add the mother's information in the same format.

c) List each child, including their full name, date and place of birth, date and place of marriage, spouse's name, and date and place of death (if applicable).

d) Include sources for each piece of information. This will save you countless headaches later!

You can create family group sheets using genealogy software (more on that in a moment) or download free templates online.

Did You Know? The largest family tree ever created contains 13 million connected individuals and was compiled by Yaniv Erlich and his colleagues at Columbia University in 2018.

Choosing your digital home: Family tree software showdown

While paper charts and family group sheets are great for getting started, you'll soon want to digitize your family tree. Digital tools offer numerous advantages:

- Easy updating and editing

- Ability to attach photos and documents
- Collaboration with other family members
- Advanced search and filtering options

Here's a quick rundown of some popular family tree software options:

a) Ancestry.com: The 800-pound gorilla of online genealogy. Pros: Huge database, intuitive interface. Cons: Subscription required for full access.

b) FamilySearch: Free, collaborative platform run by the LDS Church. Pros: Extensive records, no cost. Cons: Public tree, less control over privacy.

c) MyHeritage: User-friendly with a focus on international records. Pros: DNA integration, photo colorization tools. Cons: Subscription required for advanced features.

d) Gramps: Open-source software for the tech-savvy. Pros: Free, highly customizable. Cons: Steeper learning curve.

e) RootsMagic: Robust desktop software with online capabilities. Pros: Comprehensive features, works offline. Cons: Paid software with a learning curve.

Pro Tip: Many genealogy software options offer free trials. Test drive a few before committing to see which one fits your style and needs.

Navigating online resources: Ancestry.com, FamilySearch, and beyond

Now that you've got your digital home set up, it's time to start populating your family tree with information from online resources. Here are some key players in the online genealogy world:

a) Ancestry.com: The largest commercial genealogy website, with billions of records. Subscription required, but offers a 14-day free trial.

b) FamilySearch.org: Free site run by the LDS Church, with a vast collection of records and a collaborative family tree.

c) FindMyPast.com: Specializes in British and Irish records, but also has a growing collection of U.S. records.

d) MyHeritage.com: Strong in European records, with a user-friendly interface and DNA testing integration.

e) Newspapers.com: Massive archive of historical newspapers, great for finding obituaries and local news.

f) Fold3.com: Focuses on military records, perfect for tracing veteran ancestors.

When using these sites, keep these tips in mind:

- Start with broad searches and narrow down as you go.
- Use wildcards (* and ?) to catch spelling variations.
- Pay attention to location – many records are organized by county or parish.
- Always check the original image when available, not just the transcription.

Did You Know? Ancestry.com adds an average of 2 million records to its database every day!

Tackling brick walls: Strategies for breaking through genealogical roadblocks

Every family historian eventually hits a "brick wall" – a seemingly insurmountable obstacle in their research. Don't despair! Here are some strategies to help you break through:

a) Review your work: Sometimes the answer is hiding in plain sight. Go back and double-check your sources.

b) Broaden your search: Look for siblings, cousins, or neighbors. They might lead you back to your ancestor.

c) Consider alternate spellings: Names were often recorded phonetically, leading to creative spellings.

d) Explore different record types: If vital records are a dead end, try land records, tax lists, or church records.

e) Join a genealogy society: Local experts can offer invaluable insights and access to unique resources.

f) Take a DNA test: Genetic genealogy can open up new avenues of research and connect you with distant cousins.

g) Take a break: Sometimes, stepping away and coming back with fresh eyes can help you spot new clues.

Pro Tip: Keep a research log detailing what you've searched, where, and when. This prevents duplicating efforts and can help you spot patterns or missed opportunities.

Chapter Summary:

- Start building your family tree with what you know and interview relatives for more information.
- Use family group sheets to organize your findings.
- Choose a digital platform to store and grow your family tree.
- Utilize online resources like Ancestry.com and FamilySearch to expand your research.
- Employ various strategies to break through genealogical brick walls.

Remember, building your family tree is a marathon, not a sprint. Enjoy the journey, celebrate each discovery, and don't be afraid to reach out to the genealogy community for help. Happy ancestor hunting!

Now, let's move on to Chapter 4.

Chapter 4: Document Detectives - Unearthing Your Ancestral Paper Trail

Welcome to the thrilling world of genealogical sleuthing! In this chapter, we're going to transform you into a document detective, capable of tracking down even the most elusive ancestors. Think of yourself as a historical CSI agent, piecing together the story of your family's past through the clues left behind in various records. Let's dive into the fascinating world of genealogical documents and discover how to unearth your ancestral paper trail.

Birth, marriage, and death records: The holy trinity of genealogy

These three types of records form the backbone of genealogical research. They're often referred to as BMD (Birth, Marriage, Death) or vital records, and for good reason – they're vital to your family history quest!

a) Birth Records: Birth records typically include:

- Full name of the child
- Date and place of birth
- Parents' names (including mother's maiden name)
- Father's occupation

Pro Tip: In the U.S., statewide birth registration wasn't common until the early 1900s. For earlier births, look for church baptismal records or family Bible entries.

b) Marriage Records: Marriage records often provide:

- Names of the bride and groom

- Date and place of marriage
- Ages of the couple
- Parents' names
- Witnesses' names

Did You Know? The oldest recorded marriage certificate dates back to 1667 in Massachusetts!

c) Death Records: Death records typically include:

- Name of the deceased
- Date and place of death
- Cause of death
- Age at death
- Parents' names
- Informant's name (often a close relative)

Pro Tip: Death certificates are often the most detailed of the vital records, as they're filled out at the end of a person's life when more information is known.

To access these records:

1. Start with online databases like FamilySearch.org (free) or Ancestry.com (subscription required).
2. Check state and county vital records offices for more recent records.
3. For older records, look into church archives or local historical societies.

Remember, privacy laws vary by location. In the U.S., birth records are typically restricted for 75-100 years, marriage records for 50 years, and death records for 25-50 years.

Census records: Snapshots of your family through time

Census records are like time machines, allowing you to peek into your ancestors' lives every 10 years (in the U.S. and UK). They're invaluable for tracking families over time and discovering new family members.

Key information found in census records:

- Names of household members
- Ages and birthplaces
- Occupations
- Relationships to the head of household
- Immigration years (in some U.S. censuses)
- Property ownership

Did You Know? The 1890 U.S. Census was largely destroyed in a fire in 1921, creating a significant gap in genealogical records known as "the 1890 gap."

Tips for using census records effectively: a) Start with the most recent census and work backwards. b) Pay attention to neighbors – they might be relatives. c) Look for variations in name spellings and ages. d) Use other household members to confirm you've found the right family. e) Check every column – sometimes the most interesting details are hidden in unexpected places.

Pro Tip: The 1940 U.S. Census includes a wealth of information about the Great Depression era, including income and education levels.

Military records: Honoring your warrior ancestors

Military records can provide a wealth of information about your ancestors who served, including physical descriptions, next of kin, and details about their service.

Types of military records to explore: a) Draft registration cards b) Enlistment records c) Service records d) Pension files e) Veterans' grave registrations

Did You Know? The U.S. World War I draft registration cards include nearly 24 million men born between 1873 and 1900, even if they never served!

Where to find military records:

- Fold3.com (subscription required)
- National Archives (archives.gov)
- State archives for militia and National Guard records

Pro Tip: Pension files often contain the most genealogical information, as applicants had to prove their relationship to the veteran.

Immigration and naturalization records: Tracing your family's journey

For many of us, our ancestors' immigration stories are a crucial part of our family history. Immigration and naturalization records can help you discover when and how your family arrived in their new home.

Key immigration records: a) Passenger lists b) Border crossing records c) Naturalization petitions d) Alien registration forms

Information you might find:

- Name and age of immigrant
- Last place of residence
- Destination in the new country
- Name of ship and date of arrival
- Names of family members traveling together

Did You Know? Ellis Island processed over 12 million immigrants between 1892 and 1954. You can search their records for free at libertyellisfoundation.org.

Tips for immigration research:

- Know the approximate year of immigration (census records can help with this).
- Be prepared for name changes or creative spellings.
- Look for entire family groups traveling together.
- Check both departure and arrival lists.

Pro Tip: Naturalization records after 1906 tend to be more detailed and standardized, often including photos and physical descriptions.

Wills and probate records: Following the money (and the drama)

Wills and probate records can offer fascinating insights into your ancestors' lives, relationships, and possessions. They're also great for confirming family relationships.

What you might find in probate records:

- Names of spouse and children
- Descriptions of property and possessions
- Dates of death
- Names of executors and witnesses

- Sometimes, juicy family drama!

Did You Know? The oldest known written will dates back to 2548 BCE in ancient Egypt!

Where to find probate records:

- FamilySearch.org has a large collection of digitized probate records
- County courthouses often hold original probate files
- State archives may have microfilmed copies

Pro Tip: Even if your ancestor didn't leave a will, there might still be probate records. Look for intestate proceedings or estate inventories.

Newspaper archives: Your ancestors' 15 minutes of fame

Newspapers can provide colorful details about your ancestors' lives that you won't find in official records. They're also great for filling in gaps when other records are missing.

What to look for in newspapers: a) Obituaries b) Marriage announcements c) Birth announcements d) Local news items e) Legal notices f) Social columns

Did You Know? The oldest continuously published newspaper in the U.S. is The Hartford Courant, which began publication in 1764!

Where to find historical newspapers:

- Newspapers.com (subscription required)
- Chronicling America (free, from the Library of Congress)
- State historical society archives

- Local libraries often have microfilm collections of local papers

Tips for newspaper research:

- Be creative with name spellings and variations.
- Look for events around important dates (births, marriages, deaths).
- Don't ignore small town papers – they often included more local gossip!
- Check papers from neighboring towns and counties.

Pro Tip: Social columns in small-town newspapers can be goldmines of information about your ancestors' daily lives and social connections.

As you embark on your document detective journey, remember these key principles:

1. Always record your sources. Future you (and other researchers) will thank you.
2. Don't trust everything you read. Cross-reference information across multiple sources when possible.
3. Context is key. Understanding the historical and social context of the records you're examining can provide valuable insights.
4. Be patient and persistent. Sometimes the record you need is hiding in the last place you'd think to look.
5. Celebrate every discovery, no matter how small. Each piece of information brings you closer to understanding your family's story.

Chapter Summary:

- Vital records (birth, marriage, death) form the foundation of genealogical research.
- Census records provide snapshots of families over time.
- Military records can offer detailed information about ancestors who served.
- Immigration and naturalization records help trace your family's journey to a new country.
- Wills and probate records offer insights into family relationships and possessions.
- Newspaper archives can provide colorful details about your ancestors' lives and communities.

Remember, every document you uncover is a piece of your family's unique puzzle. Happy sleuthing, document detectives!

Chapter 5: Beyond the Basics - Advanced Genealogy Techniques

Welcome to the big leagues, genealogy rockstars! You've mastered the basics, and now it's time to level up your family history game. In this chapter, we'll dive into advanced techniques that will transform you from a casual ancestor hunter into a bona fide time-traveling detective. So grab your metaphorical deerstalker hat and magnifying glass – it's time to crack some genealogical cold cases!

Paleography: Deciphering old handwriting like a pro

Ever stared at a centuries-old document, convinced it was written by a drunken spider dipped in ink? You're not alone. Welcome to the world of paleography – the art of reading old handwriting.

Paleography is like learning a new language, except this language changes every few decades and was written by people who apparently never heard of consistent spelling. But fear not! With practice, you'll be decoding these historical puzzles faster than you can say "ye olde family tree."

Here are some tips to get you started:

- Familiarize yourself with common letter forms from different time periods. The letter 's' in particular loves to masquerade as an 'f'.
- Look for patterns in the writer's style. Once you crack their personal code, the rest becomes easier.
- Context is key. If you're reading a birth record, you know to expect certain words and phrases.

- Practice, practice, practice! The more you read, the better you'll get.

Did You Know? The word "ye" as in "ye olde shoppe" was never actually pronounced "yee." The 'y' was a representation of the Old English letter "thorn" (þ), which made a "th" sound. So "ye" was just another way of writing "the."

Cluster research: Using your ancestors' FAN club to break through brick walls

Ever hit a genealogical brick wall so hard you considered taking up a less frustrating hobby, like herding cats? Enter cluster research, also known as the FAN principle – Friends, Associates, and Neighbors. This technique is based on the radical notion that your ancestors didn't live in a vacuum (unless they were particularly antisocial time travelers).

Here's how it works:

1. Identify your ancestor's FAN club: Who were their friends, associates, and neighbors?
2. Research these people as thoroughly as you would your own ancestors.
3. Look for connections, patterns, and shared events.
4. Use this information to fill in gaps in your ancestor's story or find new leads.

For example, let's say you can't find your great-great-grandfather's birthplace. But you notice he always lived near the same three families. Research those families, and you might discover they all came from the same small village in Ireland. Bingo! You've just found a strong lead on your ancestor's origins.

DNA painting: Visualizing your genetic inheritance

DNA painting is like creating a genetic masterpiece, with you as the canvas. This technique allows you to visualize which segments of your DNA came from which ancestors. It's like a family tree, but instead of names and dates, you're looking at chromosomes and centimorgans.

Here's a quick rundown:

1. Take a DNA test (if you haven't already).
2. Identify DNA matches who share a known common ancestor with you.
3. Use a tool like DNA Painter to "paint" the segments you share with these matches onto a visual representation of your chromosomes.
4. Over time, you'll build up a colorful map showing which parts of your DNA came from which ancestral lines.

This technique can help you:

- Identify unknown matches
- Confirm paper trail research
- Spot patterns in your genetic inheritance

Did You Know? On average, you inherit about 25% of your DNA from each grandparent. But due to the random nature of genetic recombination, the actual percentage can vary widely. You might share as little as 18% or as much as 32% with any given grandparent!

Genetic genealogy databases: Maximizing your DNA test results

Remember when finding long-lost cousins required scouring phone books and pestering elderly relatives? Those days are gone, thanks to the miracle of genetic genealogy databases. These digital treasure troves allow you to compare your DNA with millions of other testers, potentially connecting you with relatives you never knew existed.

Here are some tips to make the most of these databases:

1. Test with multiple companies. Each database has a unique pool of testers.
2. Upload your raw DNA data to third-party sites like GEDmatch for even more matches.
3. Learn to use chromosome browsers and shared cM tools to analyze your matches.
4. Don't neglect your matches' family trees. They might have information you're missing.
5. Be patient. New matches appear all the time as more people test.

Remember, genetic genealogy is a team sport. The more people who test and share their results, the more we all benefit. So encourage your family members to test too!

Genealogy software: Power tools for serious family historians

If you're still keeping track of your family tree with pen and paper, it's time to join the 21st century (or at least the late 20th). Modern genealogy software is like having a personal research assistant, librarian, and organizing guru all rolled into one.

Here are some features to look for in good genealogy software:

- Easy data entry and editing
- Ability to generate various charts and reports
- Source citation tools
- Media management for photos and documents
- Web integration for easy online research
- DNA tools for managing genetic matches

Popular options include:

- Family Tree Maker
- RootsMagic
- Legacy Family Tree

Experiment with free trials to find the software that fits your needs and workflow best. Remember, the best genealogy software is the one you'll actually use consistently.

Citing sources: Because "I found it on the internet" doesn't cut it

- I know, I know. Citing sources is about as exciting as watching paint dry. But trust me, future you (and future genealogists) will thank present you for being meticulous about documentation. Plus, properly cited sources give your research credibility and allow others to verify your findings.

Here's why source citation matters:

- It allows you to retrace your steps and find information again.
- It helps you evaluate the reliability of your information.
- It gives credit to the original creators of records and research.

- It enables others to verify and build upon your work.

When citing sources, include:

- Author or creator of the record
- Title of the record or collection
- Publication information (if applicable)
- Where you found the record (archive, website, etc.)
- Date you accessed the record

Pro tip: Many genealogy software programs have built-in citation tools that make this process much easier. Use them!

Did You Know? The most comprehensive guide to genealogical source citation is "Evidence Explained" by Elizabeth Shown Mills. At over 800 pages, it's not light reading, but it's an invaluable resource for serious genealogists.

Chapter Summary:

- Paleography is the art of reading old handwriting. Practice and familiarity with historical letter forms are key.
- Cluster research involves studying your ancestors' Friends, Associates, and Neighbors to break through brick walls.
- DNA painting allows you to visualize which segments of your DNA came from which ancestors.
- Genetic genealogy databases can connect you with previously unknown relatives and confirm paper trail research.
- Genealogy software streamlines research, organization, and documentation processes.
- Proper source citation is crucial for credibility, verification, and future research.

Remember, these advanced techniques are tools in your genealogical toolkit. The more you practice and experiment with them, the more effective your research will become. Happy hunting, time travelers!

Chapter 6: Time Travel on a Budget - Genealogy Tourism 101

Pack your bags, genealogy adventurers! It's time to follow in your ancestors' footsteps – literally. In this chapter, we'll explore the exciting world of heritage travel, where history comes alive and family legends become tangible realities. But don't worry, we'll show you how to do it without breaking the bank. After all, your ancestors probably didn't travel first-class, so why should you?

Planning your heritage trip: From ancestor's doorstep to historical society

The key to a successful (and budget-friendly) genealogy trip is planning. Here's how to get started:

a) Choose your destination:

- Focus on places where multiple ancestors lived to maximize your research potential.
- Consider the accessibility of records and historical sites in the area.

b) Set clear research goals:

- What specific information are you hoping to find?
- Which ancestors or family lines will you focus on?

c) Do your homework:

- Research local archives, libraries, and historical societies before you go.
- Contact these institutions in advance to confirm hours, access policies, and any fees.

d) Create a flexible itinerary:

- Allow time for unexpected discoveries (and inevitable research dead-ends).
- Balance research time with visits to historical sites and ancestral locations.

e) Budget wisely:

- Look for off-season travel deals.
- Consider staying at budget-friendly accommodations like hostels or Airbnbs.
- Pack lunches to save on food costs during research days.

Did You Know? Many libraries and archives offer free or discounted admission to out-of-town researchers. Always ask about researcher rates when planning your visit!

Cemetery sleuthing: Grave matters and how to navigate them

Cemeteries are genealogical gold mines, offering a wealth of information etched in stone. But cemetery research requires more than just wandering around reading headstones (though that can be fun too!). Here's how to make the most of your graveyard adventures:

a) Locate the right cemetery:

- Use online resources like Find A Grave or BillionGraves to pinpoint where your ancestors are buried.
- Check multiple sources, as some older burials may not be listed online.

b) Prepare for your visit:

- Bring a cemetery kit including: a small brush for cleaning stones, non-abrasive cleaning supplies, a mirror for reflecting sunlight onto hard-to-read inscriptions, and a camera.
- Wear appropriate clothing and footwear for potentially uneven terrain.

c) Navigate the grounds:

- Look for a cemetery office or caretaker who might have maps or additional records.
- Many cemeteries have sections organized by religion, ethnicity, or time period. Familiarize yourself with the layout.

d) Interpret the stones:

- Look beyond just names and dates. Symbols, epitaphs, and even the stone material itself can provide clues about your ancestors.
- Remember that older stones may use different date conventions or abbreviations.

e) Document everything:

- Take clear photos of the headstones and surrounding area.
- Make detailed notes including the exact location of the grave.

Remember, always be respectful in cemeteries. Follow any posted rules, and never do anything that could damage the headstones or disturb other visitors.

Local archives: Treasure troves off the beaten path

While big national archives are great, don't overlook the potential goldmine of local archives. These smaller institutions often house unique records that haven't been digitized or widely shared. Here's how to make the most of your local archive visit:

a) Identify relevant archives:

- Look for county courthouses, town halls, local historical societies, and even church archives in your ancestral area.
- Don't forget about university libraries, which often have special collections related to local history.

b) Prepare in advance:

- Contact the archive to learn about access policies, hours, and any fees.
- Ask about specific collections that might be relevant to your research.
- Bring appropriate ID and any required research credentials.

c) Maximize your time:

- Make a prioritized list of records you want to check.
- Familiarize yourself with the archive's organization system before diving in.
- Bring a laptop or tablet for quick note-taking.

d) Think outside the box:

- Look for non-traditional sources like local newspapers, business records, or school yearbooks.

- Ask about vertical files or subject files, which might contain unique local history information.

e) Build relationships:

- Chat with the archivists. They often have extensive knowledge about local history and might point you towards resources you hadn't considered.
- Consider volunteering or donating to support the archive's work.

Did You Know? Many local archives rely heavily on volunteers. Offering your time to help with digitization or indexing projects can be a great way to give back to the genealogy community and potentially gain special access to records!

Connecting with distant cousins: Making new friends in old places

One of the most rewarding aspects of genealogy tourism is the opportunity to connect with living relatives. Here's how to find and reach out to distant cousins:

a) Identify potential relatives:

- Use DNA matching tools on sites like Ancestry or MyHeritage.
- Look for people researching the same family lines on genealogy forums.
- Check local phone directories or social media for people with your ancestral surnames.

b) Make initial contact:

- Craft a friendly, concise introduction explaining your relationship and research interests.
- Be clear about your intentions for connecting.

- Offer to share information you've already gathered.

c) Plan a meet-up:

- Suggest a public place for your first meeting, like a local café or library.
- Bring copies of family photos or documents to share.
- Prepare some specific questions, but also be ready to listen to their family stories.

d) Be a good guest:

- If you're invited to their home, bring a small gift (bonus points if it's related to your shared family history).
- Respect their time and privacy. Not everyone will want to dive as deep into family history as you do.

e) Maintain the connection:

- Follow up with a thank-you note or email.
- Offer to stay in touch and share future discoveries.

Remember, these are real people, not just branches on your family tree. Approach these connections with genuine interest in building relationships, not just gathering information.

Documenting your journey: Creating a genealogy travel journal

Your genealogy trip is more than just a research expedition – it's a personal journey of discovery. Keeping a detailed travel journal will help you remember the experience and potentially provide valuable context for future researchers. Here's how to create a compelling genealogy travel journal:

a) Choose your medium:

- Traditional notebook and pen
- Digital journal app on your phone or tablet
- Blog or social media posts
- Video diary

b) Record the basics:

- Dates and locations
- People you meet
- Documents you find
- Research successes (and frustrations)

c) Go beyond the facts:

- Describe the sights, sounds, and even smells of the places you visit.
- Record your emotions and reactions to discoveries.
- Sketch or photograph interesting locations or objects.

d) Include context:

- Note how the local area has changed (or stayed the same) since your ancestors' time.
- Record local customs or traditions that might have influenced your family.

e) Reflect and connect:

- How does visiting these places change your understanding of your family history?
- What new questions or research ideas have emerged from your trip?

Pro tip: Consider creating a shareable version of your journal to inspire other family members to explore their roots!

Virtual time travel: Exploring your ancestral homeland from your couch

Can't afford a plane ticket to the old country? No problem! Thanks to the wonders of technology, you can now explore your ancestral homeland without leaving your living room. Here's how:

a) Use Google Earth and Street View:

- "Walk" the streets of your ancestors' hometown.
- View historical imagery to see how places have changed over time.

b) Take virtual museum tours:

- Many museums offer online exhibitions and virtual tours.
- Look for museums focusing on local history or specific ethnic groups.

c) Attend online genealogy conferences and webinars:

- Learn from experts about researching in specific regions.
- Connect with other researchers interested in the same areas.

d) Explore digital archives:

- Many archives now offer extensive online collections.
- Look for digitized newspapers, city directories, and historical maps.

e) Join location-specific genealogy groups:

- Facebook and other social media platforms have groups dedicated to genealogy in specific regions.

- Engage with locals who can provide insights and maybe even look up information for you.

f) Use language learning apps:

- Start learning the language of your ancestral homeland.
- Understanding even basic phrases can help with future research and travel.

Did You Know? The FamilySearch website offers virtual tours of many of its worldwide family history centers. You can explore resources and get research tips without leaving home!

Chapter Summary:

- Careful planning is key to a successful and budget-friendly genealogy trip.
- Cemetery research requires preparation, respect, and attention to detail.
- Local archives often contain unique, undigitized records crucial for family history research.
- Connecting with distant cousins can provide valuable information and meaningful relationships.
- Keeping a detailed travel journal enhances your genealogy tourism experience and preserves it for future generations.
- Virtual tools allow for extensive exploration of ancestral homelands without the cost of physical travel.

Whether you're jetting off to a far-flung ancestral village or exploring your family's roots from your living room, remember that genealogy tourism is about more than just collecting facts. It's about walking in your ancestors' footsteps, understanding their world, and connecting with your heritage in a deeply personal way. So pack your bags (real or virtual), and get ready for the adventure of a lifetime!

Chapter 7: Preserving Your Legacy - From Dusty Attics to Digital Archives

In the world of genealogy, there's a saying: "A family tree without documentation is mythology." As you've delved deeper into your family's history, you've likely accumulated a treasure trove of documents, photos, and heirlooms. But how do you ensure that these precious pieces of your family's story survive for future generations? Welcome to the art and science of preserving your genealogical legacy.

Digitizing family heirlooms: Scanners, cameras, and best practices

Let's start with the basics: getting those physical artifacts into the digital realm. Whether you're dealing with fragile documents, faded photographs, or three-dimensional objects, there's a digitization method that's right for the job.

For documents and photos:

- Invest in a good flatbed scanner. Look for one with at least 600 dpi resolution for crisp, clear scans.
- Use the highest resolution possible for your scans. Remember, you can always downsize a high-resolution image, but you can't add detail to a low-res scan.
- Scan in color, even for black and white photos. This captures subtle tones and details that might be lost in grayscale.

For 3D objects:

- Use a high-quality digital camera or smartphone with a good camera.
- Set up a simple light box or use natural, diffused light to avoid harsh shadows.
- Take multiple shots from different angles to capture all details.

Best practices:

- Handle items with clean, dry hands or wear cotton gloves.
- Create a consistent file naming system. For example: "YYYY-MM-DD_LastName_FirstName_ItemDescription"
- Save files in multiple formats: TIFF for archival purposes, JPEG for sharing.

Did You Know? The Library of Congress recommends scanning most documents at 300-600 dpi, but suggests up to 1200 dpi for small or highly detailed items like postage stamps.

Oral history projects: Capturing living memories before it's too late

There's an urgency to oral history that can't be overstated. Every day, we lose irreplaceable firsthand accounts of family and historical events. But with some preparation and the right tools, you can preserve these priceless memories.

Equipment:

- A good quality digital audio recorder or smartphone with a recording app
- An external microphone for clearer sound
- A quiet, comfortable space for the interview

Interview tips:

- Prepare open-ended questions in advance, but be flexible.
- Start with basic biographical information and work towards specific memories or stories.
- Be patient and allow for pauses and tangents – sometimes the best stories come from unexpected directions.
- Consider video recording as well, to capture facial expressions and gestures.

Post-interview:

- Transcribe the interview as soon as possible while details are fresh in your mind.
- Consider using AI-powered transcription services like Otter.ai or Rev.com to save time.
- Share the transcript with the interviewee for fact-checking and additional details.
- Writing your family history: From dry facts to compelling narratives

You've gathered the facts, now it's time to breathe life into your family's story. Writing a family history isn't just about recording dates and places – it's about creating a narrative that will engage and inspire future generations.

Getting started:

- Choose a focus: A single ancestor, a family line, or a specific time period.
- Create an outline to organize your information.
- Start with a compelling hook – a dramatic event, a family mystery, or an intriguing character.

Writing tips:

- Use historical context to bring your ancestors' world to life.

- Include sensory details to make scenes more vivid.
- Balance facts with storytelling – use your research to inform your narrative, but don't be afraid to imagine details (just be clear about what's fact and what's speculation).
- Consider using creative nonfiction techniques like dialogue and scene-setting.

Editing and revising:

- Get feedback from family members and fellow genealogists.
- Fact-check rigorously – one inaccuracy can undermine your entire work.
- Consider hiring a professional editor for a final polish.
- Self-publishing options: Sharing your story with the world

Once you've written your family history, you'll want to share it. Self-publishing has never been easier or more accessible. Here are some options to consider:

Print-on-demand services:

- Amazon's Kindle Direct Publishing (KDP) offers both ebook and paperback options.
- IngramSpark is a good choice if you want your book available to bookstores and libraries.
- Lulu and Blurb are great for photo-heavy books or unique formats.

Ebook-only platforms:

- Smashwords distributes to multiple ebook retailers.
- Draft2Digital offers formatting services and wide distribution.

Traditional printing:

- Local print shops can be a good option for small runs.
- Offset printing becomes cost-effective for larger quantities (usually 500+ copies).

Considerations:

- ISBN (International Standard Book Number) – you'll need one for each format of your book.
- Copyright – your work is automatically copyrighted when written, but registering provides additional legal protections.
- Marketing – even self-published books need promotion to find readers.

1. Digital preservation: Ensuring your research outlives you

In the digital age, preserving your research isn't just about physical artifacts – it's about ensuring your digital files remain accessible and intact for generations to come.

File formats:

- Use open, widely-supported formats like PDF, TIFF, and WAV for long-term preservation.
- Avoid proprietary formats that may become obsolete.

Storage:

- Follow the 3-2-1 rule: 3 copies, 2 different media types, 1 off-site backup.
- Consider cloud storage services like Dropbox, Google Drive, or genealogy-specific options like Forever.com.

- Regularly check and update your backups – data degradation is a real concern.

Future-proofing:

- Document your organization system and passwords.
- Consider appointing a "digital executor" in your will to manage your digital legacy.

Did You Know? The average lifespan of a hard drive is only 3-5 years. Regular backups and replacements are crucial for long-term data preservation.

Ethical considerations: Navigating family secrets and sensitive information

As you delve into your family's past, you may uncover information that's sensitive, controversial, or even potentially harmful. Handling this information ethically requires careful consideration.

Privacy concerns:

- Be cautious about sharing information about living individuals without their consent.
- Consider the potential impact of revealing family secrets on living relatives.

Handling sensitive information:

- Verify information from multiple sources before including it in your family history.
- Present controversial topics objectively, providing context and avoiding judgment.
- Consider using pseudonyms or omitting names for recent, sensitive events.

Cultural sensitivity:

- Be aware of cultural differences in how family history is viewed and shared.
- Respect tribal or indigenous protocols regarding ancestral information.

Legal considerations:

- Familiarize yourself with copyright laws, especially when using photos or documents created by others.
- Be aware of defamation laws if writing about living individuals or recent events.

Remember, the goal is to preserve and honor your family's history, not to cause harm or discord. When in doubt, err on the side of discretion and respect for privacy.

Chapter Summary:

- Digitize family heirlooms using high-quality scanners and cameras, following best practices for preservation.
- Conduct oral history interviews to capture living memories, using proper equipment and techniques.
- Write your family history as a compelling narrative, balancing facts with storytelling.
- Explore self-publishing options to share your family's story with a wider audience.
- Implement robust digital preservation strategies to ensure your research survives for future generations.
- Navigate ethical considerations carefully when dealing with sensitive information and family secrets.

By following these guidelines, you're not just preserving your family's past – you're creating a legacy that will inform and inspire generations to come. Remember, every family's story is unique and valuable. Your efforts to document and share that story are a gift to your ancestors, your living relatives, and all those yet to come.

Chapter 8: Genealogy 2.0 - Leveraging Technology and Community

Welcome to the cutting edge of family history research. In this chapter, we'll explore how modern technology and online communities are revolutionizing the way we discover, share, and analyze our genealogical data. Buckle up – we're about to take your research into hyperdrive.

Social media for genealogists: Harnessing the power of crowdsourcing

Social media isn't just for sharing cat videos and vacation photos. For genealogists, it's a powerful tool for connecting with distant relatives, breaking through brick walls, and tapping into the collective knowledge of the genealogy community.

Facebook:

- Join genealogy-focused groups for specific regions, surnames, or research techniques.
- Create a family group to share discoveries and collaborate with relatives.
- Use Facebook's search function to find people with your ancestors' names or from specific locations.

Twitter:

- Follow genealogy experts and organizations for the latest news and tips.
- Use hashtags like #Genealogy, #FamilyHistory, or #AncestryHour to join conversations.

- Participate in Twitter chats like #genchat for real-time discussions.

Instagram:

- Share photos of ancestors, documents, or research finds.
- Use hashtags to reach a wider audience and connect with other researchers.
- Follow accounts that share historical photos or documents from your areas of interest.

Pinterest:

- Create boards to organize research resources, tips, and inspiration.
- Find and share infographics on genealogy topics.

LinkedIn:

- Connect with professional genealogists and archivists.
- Join genealogy-focused groups for networking and knowledge sharing.

Best practices:

- Always verify information found on social media with primary sources.
- Be cautious about sharing sensitive information about living individuals.
- Engage regularly and contribute to the community – genealogy social media works best as a two-way street.

Did You Know? The largest genealogy-focused Facebook group, "Genealogy Tip of the Day," has over 100,000 members sharing advice and breaking through brick walls together.

Genealogy podcasts and webinars: Continuing education for family historians

The world of genealogy is constantly evolving, with new resources, techniques, and technologies emerging all the time. Podcasts and webinars offer a convenient and often free way to stay up-to-date and continue your genealogical education.

Top genealogy podcasts:

1. Extreme Genes
2. Genealogy Gems
3. The Genealogy Guys
4. Research Like a Pro

Webinar providers:

- FamilySearch
- Legacy Family Tree Webinars
- National Genealogical Society

Tips for getting the most out of podcasts and webinars:

- Create a listening/viewing schedule to stay consistent.
- Take notes or create action items for each episode.
- Participate in live webinars to ask questions directly.
- Consider subscribing to premium content for in-depth learning.

1. Collaborative research: Online forums and genealogy societies

Two heads are better than one, and in genealogy, thousands of heads can be a game-changer. Online forums and genealogy societies provide platforms for collaboration, problem-solving, and shared discovery.

Online forums:

- Rootsweb mailing lists (now hosted by Ancestry)
- Genealogy Stack Exchange
- Reddit's r/Genealogy

Genealogy societies:

- National Genealogical Society
- Federation of Genealogical Societies
- International Society of Genetic Genealogy

Benefits of participation:

- Access to local expertise and resources
- Opportunities for mentorship
- Collaborative projects and indexing initiatives
- Conferences and workshops for in-person networking

Best practices for online collaboration:

- Clearly state your research question or goal.
- Provide as much relevant information as possible.
- Be open to different perspectives and approaches.
- Always verify information independently, even from trusted sources.
- Give back by helping others when you can.

1. Citizen archivists: Contributing to global genealogy projects

Want to make a lasting contribution to the genealogy community while potentially advancing your own research? Become a citizen archivist! Many organizations rely on volunteers to transcribe, index, and digitize historical records, making them accessible to researchers worldwide.

Major citizen archivist projects:

- FamilySearch Indexing
- Ancestry World Archives Project
- National Archives Citizen Archivist Dashboard
- Zooniverse's Old Weather project

Benefits of participation:

- Improve your paleography (old handwriting) skills.
- Gain intimate knowledge of various record types.
- Contribute to the preservation and accessibility of historical records.
- Potentially gain early or free access to newly digitized collections.

Getting started:

1. Choose a project that aligns with your interests or research areas.
2. Complete any required training or tutorials.
3. Start with small, manageable tasks to build confidence.
4. Set realistic goals for your volunteer time.

Did You Know? FamilySearch volunteers have indexed over 1 billion records since 2006, making these records searchable for researchers around the world.

Genetic genealogy tools: The cutting edge of DNA research

DNA testing has revolutionized genealogy, offering new ways to confirm paper trails, break through brick walls, and discover unknown relatives. But the real power of genetic genealogy lies in the analysis tools that help you make sense of your raw data.

Essential genetic genealogy tools:

- GEDmatch: A free site for uploading and comparing DNA data from multiple testing companies.
- DNA Painter: Visualize your chromosomal inheritance and map DNA segments to specific ancestors.
- Genetic Affairs: Automate the analysis of your DNA matches and cluster them into family groups.
- MyHeritage AutoClusters: Group your DNA matches into clusters to identify common ancestors.

Advanced techniques:

- Triangulation: Identifying DNA segments shared by you and at least two other matches, indicating a common ancestor.
- Chromosome mapping: Assigning specific DNA segments to particular ancestors.
- X-DNA analysis: Tracing inheritance patterns of the X chromosome for targeted research.

Ethical considerations:

- Always respect the privacy of your DNA matches.
- Be prepared for unexpected findings that may challenge your known family tree.
- Consider the potential impact of your DNA testing on other family members.

The future of family history: Emerging technologies and trends

The field of genealogy is constantly evolving, with new technologies and methodologies emerging all the time. Here's a glimpse into what the future might hold for family historians:

Artificial Intelligence (AI) and Machine Learning:

- Automated handwriting recognition for historical documents
- Intelligent matching algorithms for connecting family trees
- AI-powered colorization and enhancement of historical photos

Virtual and Augmented Reality:

- Immersive experiences of ancestral locations and historical events
- Virtual family reunions with avatars of living relatives and reconstructions of ancestors

Blockchain technology:

- Secure, decentralized storage of genealogical data
- Verifiable proof of lineage and inheritance

Advanced DNA analysis:

- Whole genome sequencing becoming more affordable and accessible
- Improved algorithms for predicting relationships and reconstructing ancestral genomes

Ethical and privacy considerations:

- Balancing the benefits of shared data with individual privacy rights
- Addressing concerns about genetic discrimination
- Developing standards for the ethical use of AI in genealogical research

As we look to the future, it's clear that technology will continue to transform the way we research and understand our family

histories. However, the core principles of good genealogy –
thorough research, careful documentation, and respect for our
ancestors and living relatives – will remain as important as ever.

Chapter Summary:

- Leverage social media platforms to connect with other researchers and break through brick walls.
- Stay updated with the latest genealogical knowledge through podcasts and webinars.
- Participate in online forums and genealogy societies for collaborative research and problem-solving.
- Contribute to global genealogy projects as a citizen archivist to give back to the community.
- Utilize cutting-edge genetic genealogy tools to maximize the value of your DNA test results.
- Stay informed about emerging technologies and trends shaping the future of family history research.

By embracing these technological advancements and community resources, you're not just researching your family history – you're actively participating in the evolution of genealogy as a field. Remember, every contribution you make, whether it's indexing a record, sharing a research tip, or solving a family mystery, helps to advance our collective understanding of the past. Happy researching, and may your family tree continue to grow and flourish in this exciting digital age!

Chapter 9: From Hobbyist to Pro - Turning Your Passion into a Career

You've caught the genealogy bug, and now you're wondering if you can turn this passion into a full-fledged career. Good news: the genealogy industry is booming, with the global genealogy products and services market expected to reach $3.4 billion by 2026(Family History: Have a Mentor? - MyHeritage Blog, n.d.). Whether you're looking to supplement your income or make a complete career change, there are numerous opportunities for those willing to put in the work and develop their skills. In this chapter, we'll explore how to transition from an enthusiastic hobbyist to a professional genealogist.

Genealogy certification: Becoming a certified genealogist

The first step in establishing yourself as a professional genealogist is to gain credibility through certification. The Board for Certification of Genealogists (BCG) offers the Certified Genealogist (CG) credential, which is widely recognized in the field(Becoming a Professional Genealogist - National Genealogical Society, n.d.).

To become certified, you'll need to:

- Meet the application requirements, including a minimum of 1,000 hours of documented genealogical research experience
- Submit a portfolio demonstrating your skills in research, analysis, and writing
- Pass a rigorous evaluation process

Did You Know? The BCG was founded in 1964 and has certified over 2,000 genealogists since its inception.

While certification is not mandatory to work as a genealogist, it can significantly boost your credibility and open doors to more opportunities. Many government agencies, law firms, and high-profile clients prefer to work with certified genealogists.

Specializing in niche markets: Finding your genealogy superpower

As you gain experience in genealogy, you'll likely discover areas where you excel or have a particular interest. Specializing in a niche can set you apart from other genealogists and make you the go-to expert in that area(Do You Know Your Niche Within The Genealogy Community?, n.d.). Some potential niches include:

- DNA testing and genetic genealogy
- Immigration research
- Military genealogy
- African American genealogy
- Jewish genealogy
- One-Name Studies
- Graveyard studies
- Heraldry

For example, Jennifer Holik specializes in WWI/WWII research and writing, as well as ancestral healing(Do You Know Your Niche Within The Genealogy Community?, n.d.). By focusing on a specific area, you can develop deep expertise and attract clients who need your specialized knowledge.

Building your brand: Marketing yourself as a genealogy expert

In today's digital age, building a strong personal brand is crucial for success as a professional genealogist. Here are some strategies to establish yourself as an expert:

a) Create a professional website: Showcase your services, expertise, and testimonials from satisfied clients.

b) Start a blog: Share your knowledge and insights regularly to demonstrate your expertise and attract potential clients.

c) Utilize social media: Platforms like LinkedIn, Facebook, and Twitter can help you connect with other genealogists and potential clients(Do You Know Your Niche Within The Genealogy Community?, n.d.).

d) Develop a unique selling proposition (USP): What makes you different from other genealogists? Perhaps it's your specialized knowledge, your research methodology, or your ability to tell compelling family stories.

e) Network actively: Attend genealogy conferences, join online forums, and participate in local genealogical societies to expand your professional network(Family History: Have a Mentor? - MyHeritage Blog, n.d.).

Freelance opportunities: Writing, research, and speaking gigs

As a professional genealogist, you can explore various freelance opportunities to diversify your income streams:

a) Writing: Contribute articles to genealogy magazines, websites, or local historical publications. You can also ghostwrite family histories for clients.

b) Research: Offer your services on freelance platforms like Upwork, where clients are actively seeking genealogists for various projects(Genealogy Jobs | Upwork™, n.d.).

c) Speaking engagements: Present at genealogy conferences, local historical societies, or libraries. Share your expertise and build your reputation as a knowledgeable speaker.

d) Consulting: Offer one-on-one consultations to help clients break through their research brick walls or interpret DNA results.

Did You Know? Many professional genealogists combine multiple income streams to create a sustainable career. For example, you might offer research services, teach online courses, and write books on genealogy topics.

Teaching genealogy: Sharing your knowledge with others

Teaching is an excellent way to establish yourself as an expert and give back to the genealogy community. Consider these teaching opportunities:

a) Online courses: Create and sell courses on platforms like Udemy or Teachable, covering topics from beginner basics to advanced research techniques.

b) Webinars: Host live or pre-recorded webinars on specific genealogy topics.

c) Local classes: Offer in-person classes at community centers, libraries, or genealogical societies.

d) One-on-one tutoring: Provide personalized instruction to help individuals improve their research skills.

Remember, teaching not only helps others but also reinforces your own knowledge and keeps you up-to-date with the latest genealogy trends and techniques.

Ethical considerations for professional genealogists

As you transition into a professional genealogist, it's crucial to adhere to ethical standards. The Association of Professional Genealogists (APG) has a Code of Ethics that all members agree to follow(Code of Ethics - Association of Professional Genealogists, n.d.). Some key ethical considerations include:

a) Communicating truthfully and accurately about your abilities and credentials.

b) Preparing clear agreements with clients regarding scope, timeframes, deliverables, and fees.

c) Maintaining confidentiality of client information and obtaining informed consent before sharing any data.

d) Complying with copyright laws, privacy regulations, and other applicable rules.

e) Treating other genealogists and the profession with respect and civility.

By adhering to these ethical standards, you'll build a reputation for professionalism and integrity, which is essential for long-term success in the field.

Chapter Summary:

- Pursue genealogy certification to establish credibility and open up more opportunities.
- Identify and develop a niche specialization to set yourself apart from other genealogists.
- Build your personal brand through a professional website, blog, and social media presence.
- Explore freelance opportunities in writing, research, and speaking engagements.
- Consider teaching genealogy through online courses, webinars, or local classes.
- Adhere to ethical standards to maintain professionalism and integrity in your work.

Now, let's move on to Chapter 10:

Chapter 10: The Never-Ending Story - Continuing Your Genealogy Journey

Congratulations! You've come a long way in your genealogy journey. But as any seasoned family historian will tell you, the quest for knowledge never truly ends. In this final chapter, we'll explore ways to keep your passion alive, continue growing as a genealogist, and give back to the community that has supported you along the way.

Joining genealogy societies: Finding your tribe

One of the best ways to stay engaged and motivated in your genealogy journey is by joining genealogy societies. These organizations offer numerous benefits, including:

a) Access to exclusive resources and databases b) Networking opportunities with fellow enthusiasts c) Regular meetings and educational events d) Collaborative research projects

Did You Know? The National Genealogical Society, founded in 1903, is one of the oldest and largest genealogical organizations in the United States, with over 9,000 members.

When choosing a society to join, consider both local and national organizations. Local societies can provide valuable insights into specific geographic areas, while national societies offer broader resources and networking opportunities

Matt Menashes, NGS executive director, emphasizes the importance of group activities in genealogy: "Group activities are part of the human experience, and that's what societies provide:

chances to learn, collaborate, socialize [and] share common interests"

Attending conferences: Genealogy's greatest hits

Genealogy conferences are like rock concerts for family history enthusiasts. They offer a unique opportunity to:

a) Learn from expert speakers and attend workshops b) Discover new research techniques and tools c) Network with fellow genealogists d) Explore vendor exhibits featuring the latest genealogy products and services

Some of the most popular annual conferences include:

- RootsTech (both in-person and virtual options)
- National Genealogical Society Family History Conference
- Federation of Genealogical Societies Conference

Did You Know? The 2023 RootsTech virtual conference attracted over 1 million participants from more than 225 countries and territories, making it the largest genealogy event in the world.

When attending conferences, come prepared with business cards, a notebook, and a plan for which sessions you want to attend. Don't be shy about introducing yourself to speakers and fellow attendees – you never know what valuable connections you might make!

Volunteering: Giving back to the genealogy community

As you progress in your genealogy journey, consider giving back to the community that has supported you. Volunteering not only helps others but also enhances your own skills and knowledge. Here are some ways to volunteer:

a) Indexing records: Many organizations, such as FamilySearch, rely on volunteers to digitize and index historical records

b) Grave documentation: Contribute to projects like Find A Grave or BillionGraves by photographing and documenting headstones in your local cemeteries

c) Local history projects: Assist your local historical society or library with organizing and preserving documents and artifacts.

d) Genealogy lookup services: Offer to do lookups in local records for researchers who can't visit in person.

e) Mentoring: Share your knowledge with beginners through local genealogy societies or online forums

Remember, volunteering is a two-way street. As you help others, you'll often discover new resources and techniques that can benefit your own research.

Mentoring newbies: Passing on the family history torch

As you gain experience and expertise, consider becoming a mentor to those just starting their genealogy journey. Mentoring not only helps newcomers but also reinforces your own knowledge and keeps you engaged in the field.

Here's how you can be an effective genealogy mentor:

a) Offer different perspectives on research problems b) Encourage mentees to find answers themselves c) Share your experiences, including mistakes you've made d) Provide guidance on using various genealogical resources e) Offer emotional support and encouragement

Did You Know? Many genealogists credit their success to the guidance of a mentor early in their journey. By mentoring others, you're continuing a long-standing tradition in the genealogy community

Setting new goals: Challenging yourself to dig deeper

To keep your genealogy journey exciting and rewarding, it's essential to set new goals and challenges for yourself. Here are some ideas:

a) Break through a long-standing brick wall in your family tree b) Learn a new language to access foreign records c) Master a new genealogy software or tool d) Write and publish a family history book e) Organize a family reunion based on your research f) Take on a One-Name Study or One-Place Study

When setting goals, use the S.M.A.R.T. framework: Specific, Measurable, Achievable, Realistic, and Time-bound. This approach will help you stay focused and motivated as you tackle new challenges.

Celebrating your achievements: Because you've earned it, genealogy rockstar!

Last but not least, don't forget to celebrate your achievements along the way. Genealogy can be a long and sometimes frustrating journey, so it's important to acknowledge your successes, no matter how small they may seem.

Here are some ways to celebrate your genealogy wins:

a) Keep a research journal to track your progress and breakthroughs b) Share your discoveries with family members or on social media c) Create a visual representation of your family tree to display d) Attend a genealogy conference or workshop as a reward for reaching a goal e) Plan a heritage trip to visit ancestral locations

Remember, every step forward in your research is an achievement worth celebrating. As you reflect on your journey, take time to practice gratitude for the resources, people, and discoveries that have enriched your life through genealogy(Practice Gratitude in Genealogy Organising - Genealogy Space, n.d.).

Chapter Summary:

- Join genealogy societies to connect with like-minded individuals and access valuable resources.
- Attend genealogy conferences to learn from experts and network with fellow enthusiasts.
- Give back to the community through volunteering and mentoring newcomers.
- Set new goals to challenge yourself and keep your genealogy journey exciting.
- Celebrate your achievements, both big and small, along the way.
- Remember that genealogy is a lifelong journey of discovery and personal growth.

Conclusion: Your Genealogy Journey - A Legacy in the Making

As we reach the end of this book, it's time to reflect on the incredible journey you've embarked upon. From those first tentative steps into your family's past to the confident strides you're now taking as a seasoned genealogist, you've uncovered stories, solved mysteries, and perhaps even rewritten your family's narrative.

Throughout this book, we've explored the many facets of genealogy research, from the basics of getting started to the advanced techniques used by professionals. Let's take a moment to recap the key points from each chapter:

1. In Chapter 1, we laid the foundation for your genealogy journey, emphasizing the importance of starting with what you know and working backwards. We discussed the value of family interviews and the need to organize your initial findings.
2. Chapter 2 introduced you to the vast world of genealogical records, from vital records to census data, and everything in between. We explored both online and offline resources, emphasizing the importance of cross-referencing and verifying information.
3. In Chapter 3, we delved into the digital age of genealogy, exploring online databases, genealogy software, and mobile apps. We discussed the pros and cons of various platforms and how to choose the right tools for your research.
4. Chapter 4 tackled the challenge of breaking through brick walls in your research. We explored advanced search techniques, the importance of lateral

thinking, and how to use indirect evidence to solve genealogical puzzles.

5. In Chapter 5, we explored the exciting world of DNA testing for genealogy. We discussed the different types of DNA tests, how to interpret your results, and ethical considerations surrounding genetic genealogy.

6. Chapter 6 took us beyond names and dates, focusing on how to add context and depth to your family history. We explored social history resources, newspaper archives, and methods for bringing your ancestors' stories to life.

7. Chapter 7 addressed the crucial topic of preserving your genealogical legacy. We discussed digitization techniques, oral history projects, and methods for sharing your research with future generations.

8. In Chapter 8, we explored the collaborative aspects of genealogy, including social media, online forums, and citizen archivist projects. We emphasized the power of community in genealogical research.

9. Chapter 9 provided guidance for those considering a transition from hobbyist to professional genealogist. We discussed certification, niche specialization, and ethical considerations for working in the field.

10. Finally, in Chapter 10, we looked at ways to continue your genealogy journey, including joining societies, attending conferences, and giving back to the community through volunteering and mentoring.

As you reflect on all you've learned, remember that genealogy is more than just a hobby or a potential career path. It's a journey of self-discovery, a way to honor your ancestors, and a means of preserving your family's legacy for future generations.

Your research has the power to:

1. Connect you with your roots and give you a sense of belonging
2. Uncover important medical information that could benefit your family
3. Correct historical inaccuracies and fill gaps in the historical record
4. Bring families closer together through shared history
5. Preserve stories and traditions that might otherwise be lost to time

As you continue your genealogy journey, keep in mind these key principles:

1. Always verify your sources and maintain high standards of accuracy
2. Be open to new information, even if it challenges your preconceptions
3. Respect the privacy of living individuals in your research
4. Collaborate with others and share your knowledge generously
5. Never stop learning and exploring new avenues of research

Remember, every family has a unique story waiting to be discovered. Your dedication to uncovering and preserving that story is a gift not only to your immediate family but to future generations and to the broader historical record.

As you move forward, set new goals for yourself. Perhaps you want to break through that stubborn brick wall, write a family history book, or even pursue certification as a professional genealogist. Whatever your aspirations, approach them with the same curiosity and determination that brought you this far.

Don't be discouraged by setbacks or dead ends in your research. Every experienced genealogist has faced challenges, and it's often these obstacles that lead to the most rewarding discoveries. Embrace the detective work, the problem-solving, and the moments of serendipity that make genealogy such a thrilling pursuit.

Take time to celebrate your achievements along the way. Whether it's finding a long-lost ancestor, connecting with a distant cousin, or simply organizing your research more effectively, each step forward is a victory